1 7 0 5 3 0 2 7 1 9

National Airport na me get am
National Stadium na me build am
President na my sister brother
You be the mugu, I be the master
Oyinbo I go chop your dollar, I go take your money disappear
419 is just a game, you are the loser I am the winner
— 'I Go Chop Your Dollar', Nkem Owoh (2005)

My ideal room mate would be:
CLEAN
Employed
Easygoing and fun, with good energy and sense of humor (if you're uptight/high-strung
  this might not be the place for you)
Working full-time, goal oriented and career driven
Independent, w/ no drama
Spiritually oriented or at least 'Karma' oriented
Amazingly kind and honest (as am I)
Non-Smoker and No Drugs (I'm flexible on the occasional '420 friendly')
Honesty, communication, and respect are a must.
— Los Angeles Craigslist > central LA > sublets & temporary
  > $800 GREAT ROOM 4 Rent

THE YOUNG MAN IS CROUCHED and intent — lost in his role, ignoring the camera. Looking at the array of photographs of attempted re-stagings of the same scene, he comes across as the ringleader, if only by virtue of the fact that he seems more prepared to give himself over, not only to the fiction he and his gang have initiated, but also to each alter ego in the command subplot suggested by his audience of one. Right now he is James Dean, crouched over a pool table in full glowering heartthrob mode. Does he remember that he is also nominally the son of the former finance minister of Nigeria — juggling a scheme to extract $60 million from the country with the assistance of his one-man audience? As he crouches to take his shot, is part of him still inhabiting the role of Elvis Aaron Presley (now being dutifully, if woodenly, channelled by another man at the opposite end of the table) from a moment ago? Or is he already preparing to be a thoughtful Humphrey Bogart, studying the game and waiting to take his turn (just as soon as Marilyn Monroe stops flirting and climbs off the table)?

For now he crouches, fingers splayed to bridge the cue — cigarette and tie hanging at precise casual angles that perfectly mimic those of the 'original' image. There's something very touching about these exact attentions to detail within the broad sketchy canvas of this generic Lagos bar and its cheap pool table, which could only ever vaguely approximate the original painting's plush American lawyer's office and luxury billiard table surrounded by iconic dead celebrities (in poses licensed from their respective estates). The intertextual in-jokes in the books and pictures that line that office's walls (references to Norma Jean Baker, filmographies posing as law books, photos of a Porsche Spyder sports car), are represented by a single counterpart here — an unfussy poster for Gulder beer over 'Bogart's' shoulder. Should we read something into this, in the spirit of the heavy-handed medieval logic of the original's iconography? Is this a reference to the Dutch guilder? To ransom demands following abductions at Schiphol airport, should the plan develop and the mark be drawn to a meeting?[1]

---

[1] The U.S. State Department routinely issues statements to travellers warning about abductions and even murders for those who are taken in by spam frauds. In order to draw the maximum amount of money from a victim, the victim must be as disorientated as possible and drawing them off their home territory is an endgame tactic — usually framed as a proposed meeting with a lawyer in Amsterdam or a similar European hub to 'finalise the deal'.

No. It's a poster advertising Gulder beer in a bar.[2] The young man's intensity and attention to detail is clearly an anomaly within the indifferently staged scene: wooden Elvis is self-consciously hunched over his cue, Marilyn appears to be smirking, and such intensity as Bogart is summoning would appear to have more to do with irritation that he didn't get to be James Dean this time round.

It's a shabby scene. I find myself wondering about the camera noise when the shot is taken.[3] It seems like the one occasion when the manufacturer's gimmick of installing an ersatz mechanical shutter sound into cheap 35mm digital cameras might be appropriate. A tinny illusion of mechanical weight to match the

---

2 Though perhaps there's a clue of sorts that all is not right. An article written by Amos Adetunji in *The Times of Lagos* in 2002 warned of a wave of counterfeiting of premium-brand beers. Brands such as Guinness, Star Beer and Gulder were being targeted in frauds where so-called second-tier beers were being rebottled and sold as their better-known counterparts. The article suggested that the government was considering enhanced laserjet or inkjet time stamping on bottles and kegs to verify the authenticity of the product. How this would actually prevent fraud seemed unclear.

3 The engineer and co-founder of EAT (Experiments in Art and Technology), Billy Kluver, carried out an elaborate project called *A Day with Picasso*, where, extrapolating from some noted similarities of clothing and lighting between photographs of the artist found in different archives, he was able not only to connect them as having been taken on the same day in 1916 but by consulting journal entries for those present and studying maps, weather reports and angles of shadows etc., to fix the exact time and place at which they were taken, by whom (Jean Cocteau) and with what model of camera. This dogged retrieval of data that would now be routinely embedded in digital imagery was successful in part because of the way it also hinted at the intimacies and intrigues as a group of friends drifted through a single day — intimacies beneath the conventional focus of the portrait lenses of the day. One has only to compare the stiffly posed portraits of Dadaists from the same year to appreciate the quality of horseplay and informality in the Cocteau photos, which Kluver has assembled in a kind of stop-frame form for us to animate with a contemporary narrative. When looking at the series of photos of the Lagos gang posing at the request of the man they are trying to con, the desire to extrapolate from any single technical detail of the construction of the image a presumed greater understanding of the milieu faces challenges not so much within locating the kind of metadata described above (and whose potential grows with every successive iteration of locative media technology, such as GPS, mobile phone applications, etc.) but in understanding the agency that brings these players in front of the camera at all, not least when a con is being enacted, when the bar for what is considered worthy of recording is lowered further and further, often in inverse proportion to the legibility of the recorded action for a viewer.

4

FEDERAL REPUBLIC OF NIGERIA
OFFICE OF THE PRESIDENT

SECRET SERVICE
★ NO FINANCIAL LOSS
FOR YOUR DATABASE★

OPF/FGN/VOL.1/00

ASO ROCK VILLA ABUJA - NIGERIA
FAX : 234-90-404361 ,TELEFAX: 234-90-489618
TEL: 234-1-7752936

PAST DUE

From the Desk of the President Olusegun M.Obasanjo

ATTN: HONOURABLE CONTRACTOR WITH THE
FEDERAL REPUBLIC OF NIGERIA

FOLLOWING THE PROMISE MADE TO THE INTERNATIONAL COMMUNITIES, OTHER INTERNATIONAL
BODIES AND ESTABLISHEMENTS, IN MY POLITICAL MONIFESTO DURING MY CAMPAIGN, TO CLEAR
AND SETTLE ALL FOREIGN CONTRACTOR TO THE FEDERAL REPUBLIC OF NIGERIA CONTRACT
PAYMENTS.

I ADVISE FOREIGN CONTRACTORS TO CONTACT DR. DICKSON DAVID (INTERNATIONAL PAYMENT
OFFICER) ON HIS PRIVATE FAX: 1 212 629 2072 TO RE-CONFIRM THE FOLLOWING:-

A. BANK ACCOUNT
B. CONTRACT VALUE
C. CONTRACT NUMBER AND OTHER RELEVANT INFORMATION THAT WILL
AID IN RECONFIRMING AND VERIFYING THEIR CONTRACT.
D. YOUR PRIVATE TELEPHONE AND FAX NUMBER.

VERY URGENT

DURING YOUR CONTACT TO THE PERSONAL ADVISER TO THE HEAD OF STATE ON FOREIGN
PAYMENT, YOU SHOULD ENDEAVOUR TO REQUEST FOR YOUR INTERNATIONAL PAYMENT RELEASE
CODE NUMBER WHICH HAS BEEN ISSUED EXCLUSIVELY FOR YOUR TRANSFER.

AGAIN, POWER AND MANDATE HAS BEEN GIVEN TO HIM TO ENABLE HIM SETTLE ALL FOREIGN
CONTRACTORS PAYMENT BEFORE THE END OF THIS FIRST QUARTER 2000 FISCAL YEAR. SO BE
HUNDRED PERCENT REST ASSURED THAT PROPER ARRANGEMENT HAS BEEN MADE TO SEE THAT
EVRY FOREIGN CONTRACTORS RECEIVES HER CONTRACT AMOUNT BEFORE THE END OF THIS
FIRST QUARTER.

FINALLY, ALL FURTHER CONTACT WITH OUR LIAISON OFFICE ABROAD AND OTHER DEPARTMENT
BY FOREIGN CONTRACTORS SHOULD BE STOPPED IMMEDIATELY TO AVOID COMPLICATIONS AND
MISAPPROPRIATION OF FUNDS.

ON BEHALF OF THE FEDERAL REPUBLIC OF NIGERIA WE REGRET ALL INCONVIENCES YOU MAY
HAVE SUFFERRED CAUSED BY THE MILITARY REGIME IN YOUR CONTRACT FUND TRANSFER, WHILE
I AM CONGRATULATING YOU IN ADVANCE, I LOOK FORWARD TO YOUR ESTABLISHING AND URGENT
CONTACT WITH DR. DICKSON DAVID (INTERNATIONAL PAYMENT OFFICER)

BEST REGARDS

DESPATCHED

JUSTICE USMAN DUNLAMI
LEGAL ADVISER TO THE PRESIDENT

TOTAL P.01

5

synthetic manner in which the pixels will flare and clump, as if in betrayal of the thin, thin fiction.

Anyway, it's done. It's what the audience wanted. The members of the gang relax, maybe order a Gulder and think about the next stage of the plan. As their American patron sleeps across the ocean, a USB cable is located to upload the images and mail them. The young man straightens up, maybe hands the tie back to the barman and moves back to another level of mask play. Once again he is wholly the son of the former finance minister of Nigeria. His father has died suddenly and has experienced a deathbed conversion in which he repented the evil done in his government's name. He has made his son promise to distribute the dirty oil money to good causes to make restitution. His mournful and blessed son needs only the bank details of a good person to ensure the money's safe passage out of the country. Alas, he has not always been so good, but now, when misfortune falls and his father confronts him with his wickedness, he sees that his father was right and must now seek goodness wherever it may fall.[4] You were recommended to him as someone whose goodness is a matter of renown and whose heart is pure for this endeavour. If you would only contact him in utmost

---

4 The melodramatic, rhetorical language that characterises Nigerian spam letters speaks to a number of traditions and movements in Nigeria in the latter half of the twentieth century, not least the extraordinary burst of publishing activity that centred in and around the Onitsha open-air market in the 1950s and 1960s, when a wave of indigenous publishing married African oral traditions with the mass interests of an emerging class of Nigerians literate in English (a lesser-known strand of Nigerian literature also developed out of the Arabic tradition) to produce penny pamphlets, often in the form of morality plays, riddles and jokes — always tailored towards the more sensational demands of the market and with many anonymous authors borrowing from each other at will. Titles such as *How to write important letters, applications, agreements and love letters* (J. Abiakam), and *Western ladies and car free lifts lead to the production of fatherless children* (Olusola Asani) are arguably direct antecedents of today's Nollywood (the nickname for the hugely prolific, low-budget Nigerian film industry) — where an underlying strict morality is extrapolated to ridiculously punitive extremes, so that routinely violent and tragic endings await those who stray from moral norms. Read in this spirit, some of the Nigerian spam letters come across like the first act of film pitches . . .

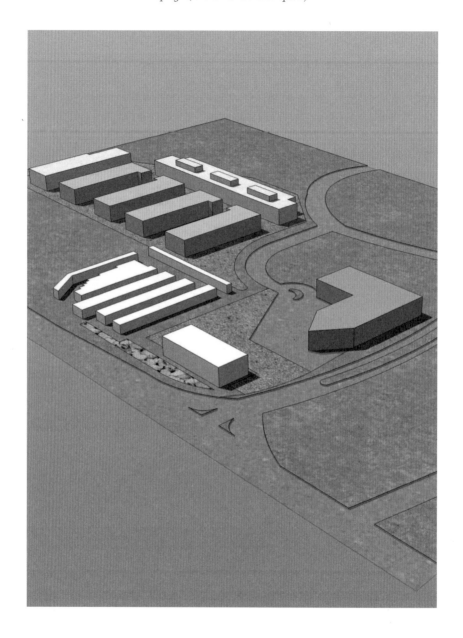

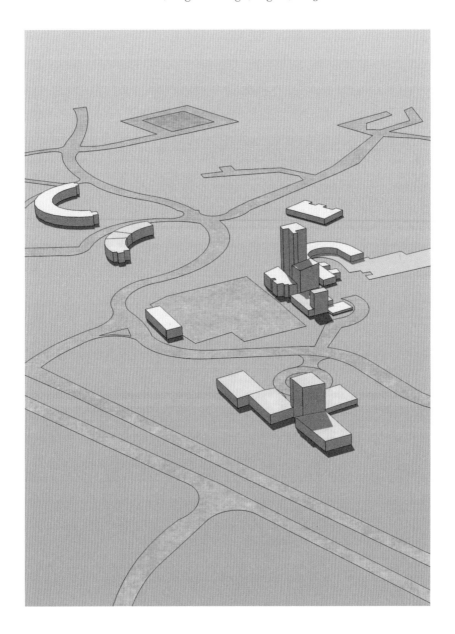

secrecy and not a word must be breathed lest the authorities find out and he be subjected to prison and torment on top of his grief . . .[5]

James Dean was more fun — a change. These other stories wear thin. The finance minister's son, the Iraqi museum looter, the Saudi businessman with cancer of the oesophagus who has now found Jesus, the German banker who died on Concorde — all these generic ciphers whose stories have been repeated wearily to the point of aphasia by this gang and hundreds of others, borrowing the same characters and storylines of doom and redemption for their florid email appeals. To the young man, they are casually interchangeable masks and speeches — the particular one he is wearing or uttering at any given moment is less important than the moment at which a remote viewer chooses to observe and respond to one of the stock routines in his latter-day Commedia dell'Arte repertoire.[6] At that

---

5 It's tempting to directly link the more archaic English terms within Nigerian spam with the history and spread of colonial English and an accompanying lag around access to changing norms in business communication — the occasional compendiums of spam that have thus far been published in the U.S. and Europe extract value from this presumed lag by suggesting that humour lies in these 'failures' within Nigerian spam letters' appeals to contemporary Western sensibilities. Interestingly, these acts of cultural recuperation are usually seen as occupying a lower rung of humourous irony than another form of cultural extraction from spam, 'poetry' performance readings of spam e-mails — performances which routinely focus on chance poetics within the computer-generated found texts that pad messages to defeat software filters. Both of the tactics being lampooned use an instrumentalising approach to language to bypass filters, be those filters human or software. Both are regarded as ridiculous from a vantage point of literate privilege. But it's interesting that the hackers' crude algorithms are seen as marginally more worthy of celebration than the Nigerian's stock melodramatic flourishes.

6 Perhaps an equally pertinent reference in this instance might be to the West African tradition of masquerade — in particular the Igbo tradition of Mmanwu (drawn from the words for *spirit* and *death*), where mask rituals would be enacted in villages for thanksgiving for harvest, for protection, etc., and where, crucially, the participants believed that the spirits of their dead ancestors were brought forth in them through the adoption of the masks during the rituals. 'As a matter of fact, no matter the effect of urbanization and modernization, Igbo masquerades are seen as spirits. This is why there is always a certain aura and mystery around the performance of a masquerade. And it makes much sense to say that the ideology of most

moment of observation the character framing the initial exchange is trans-formed. The introspection that may have marked the fictional content of their first e-mail (the appeal to an essentially private vanity and sentimentality in the reader) is dropped in favour of action and urgency: a kind of dance starts, with its tempo pressing ever faster. Financial details, signatures, deposits and bribes to ease last-minute hitches are now all demanded with increasing urgency and frequency — the promise of millions deferred endlessly as the gullible target is bled.

Occasionally, as in this case, someone will respond enthusiastically but slightly sceptically to the first overture. No matter, the young man thinks — the smarter they believe they are, the more their vanity will work to betray them.

This guy for example. American. Says he can help get the $60 million out of the country. Thinks it's terrible what the oil companies are doing to the Delta and glad the minister had such an epiphany. He has a couple of tricky questions: 'On that note you say "father" and that he'd recently died? Isn't Ngozi Okonjo-Iweala a woman, alive and incumbent for the last two years?' This is correct — it's 2005 and she will go on to be managing director of the World Bank in 2007. He queries some other points — establishes his creden-tials as a man to be taken seriously.[7] The American claims to be concerned by these details, but chiefly troubled by the idea that he might be talking to a machine generating this letter automatically. He wants to go up the chain of

---

Igbo masking is rooted in the closeness and interpenetration of the worlds of the dead and the living'(Ben Okwu Eboh, *Masquerade in Igbo Cultural Milieu: A Problem of Aesthetic Interpretation and Appreciation*). Back to the question from the first paragraph of this text — what is the young man thinking as he adopts the mask of the dead global villager James Dean over the mask of the finance minister's son? Who is he becoming in that moment? For more on mas-querade and its role within recent Nigerian literature as a mode for commentary and dissent, particularly from the Nigerian-Biafran war onwards, see the writings of Emmanuel N. Obiechina, in particular his *Language and Theme: Essays on African Literature* and *Masquerade for Our Times*.

7 These are of course the best victims, these preachers and disciples of self-reliance . . .

command, he says; he wants to know that he's speaking to a person. So he proposes a kind of Turing test.[8]

The American has sent the Nigerian an e-mail asking him to photographically re-create an attached image of a painting as confirmation that a human is reading and processing his communication. The 'photo shoot' that has just taken place is the result. It's an odd request (in spirit, somewhere between the Bayesian filtering techniques used to automatically filter spam algorithms on the one hand and some kind of misplaced due diligence from a longer history of suspect human transactions on the other), but the gang is happy to comply — any response is better than none. Get the victim talking and snare him. Hopefully he will start paying soon. As the recent Lagos club hit has it:

> *Oyinbo people greedy, I say them greedy*
> *I don see them tire thats why when them fall enter my trap o!*
> *I dey show them fire*[9]

---

8   In 1950, Alan Turing proposed a means of addressing the question of whether machines can
-   think. In and of itself, such a question was, to Turing, almost meaningless, but a question
    could be devised around how well a computer performed in something he called 'The
    Imitation Game'. The game's origins can roughly be traced back to Descartes' *Discourse on the
    Method*: 'For we can certainly conceive of a machine so constructed that it utters words, and
    even utters words that correspond to bodily actions causing a change in its organs... But it is
    not conceivable that such a machine should produce different arrangements of words so as to
    give an appropriately meaningful answer to whatever is said in its presence, as the dullest of
    men can do.' In Turing's test, a machine and a human would be placed in one room and an
    interrogator in another. The interrogator would ask the two parties a series of questions, each
    one aimed specifically at one party or the other — with the machine charged with deceiving
    the interrogator into believing they are human and the human charged with helping the inter-
    rogator reach the correct conclusion. Their responses should ideally appear as transcripts
    before the interrogator. The game finishes with the interrogator declaring one or other parties
    to be the machine and the other the human. The game is still the subject of numerous online
    competitions for chatbots and the like, and the phrase 'Turing test' has come to be applied to
    an ever broader range of human computer interactions. The test proposed by our American is
    within this latter vernacular tradition. For more information, see Graham Oppy and David Dowe,
    'The Turing Test', *The Stanford Encyclopedia of Philosophy*, Summer 2008, Edward N. Zalta (ed.),
    http://plato.stanford.edu/archives/sum2008/entries/turing-test/

The dial-up connection is shockingly slow today. Recent-Bogart is elbowing Recent-Elvis out of the way, convinced he has attached the documents wrongly, but eventually the message inches through and starts its transatlantic journey. After a number of indirect hops it will enter America via a server farm in Reston, Virginia, and make its way to the American target's inbox.

Server farms have proliferated in recent years — quietly introducing a new vernacular architectural form into the American landscape — usually in spaces where traditional industrial practices have receded and cleared capacity on the power grid. In many ways the 'farms' appear to be generic big-box architecture, often built on or near landfills in underfinanced Eastern seabord states, which will often have made agreements to dispose of the trash from, say, New York and have then doubly utilised the land by building these farms on top. They become remarkable only when you consider that the processing power that makes the Internet possible generates an extraordinary amount of heat, so that extensive and expensive cooling systems are required for buildings which might otherwise resemble a Wal-Mart store. U.S. government figures in late 2007 estimated that server farms alone consumed more than $3.3 billion in energy per year. Add to that the fact that the sleeping American's computer is contributing to an estimated national consumption level of 60,000 megawatts per hour (or, as one environmental group put it, more than twice the energy capacity of China's huge Three Gorges hydroelectric dam),[10] based on measuring *sleeping computers alone*, and it gives the lie to the myth of the Internet as somehow existing only in some ethereal sphere of abstract information. Its carbon footprints are trampled across the landscape, concealed by these banal edifices.[11] The trash ferments below and flows in bits above — each process adding layers of friction and heat.

---

9   The song 'I go chop your dollar' was recorded by the Nigerian comedian and film actor Nkem Owoh in 2005 as part of the soundtrack for the film *The Master,* which was about a 419 scammer. The song was quickly banned by the Economic and Financial Crimes Commission and the Nigerian Broadcasting Commission. Nkem Owoh was arrested in Amsterdam on suspicion of participation in an online lottery fraud in June 2007.

10 Estimate by Zerofootprint cited in *Sydney Morning Herald,* January 8, 2008.

So the Nigerian's message passes through this building over the landfill, and the next morning, having deleted the day's fresh supply of spam and gone through the replies to his online ad for a roommate, the American gets to see the low-resolution JPEGs of the spam-gang-member-as-Nigerian-finance-minister's-son-as-James-Dean.

The American examines the careful look of concentration on the face of the James Dean figure, looks back at the original image of Chris Consani's painting *Legal Action* and bursts out laughing . . .

Unfortunately for the Nigerian gang, the American is not a rich, elderly newcomer to the Internet or a town treasurer in a personal cash crunch or indeed any of the other archetypal victims of this particular form of wire fraud — archetypes both as quasi-mythical and as necessary to the fraud as any of the implausible figures sketched by the Nigerian gangs. Instead he is a 'scambaiter' — someone whose vanity is directed not into a desperate belief in a 'too-good-to-be-true' offer, but towards a celebration of his own literacy in the ways of the online con and a self-justified delight in turning the tables on his would-be tormentors. The original mail or fax from the Nigerian gang, as described above, is a classic attempt at a so-called 419 scam (named for a numbered provision in the Nigerian penal code that relates to such frauds). Electronic versions of this con began proliferating on Usenet boards and inboxes in the mid to late 1990s — though the trope of the con they describe can be traced through the rag and wire frauds of railroad-era America and in letter form from long before even that. By 2005, when the American receives the particular message he chose to respond to, this particular con has long since become a familiar idiomatic inbox nuisance, and 419 has become a catch-all term for all sorts of letter frauds. And

---

11 As noted, the transformation is stealthy and its initial manifestations seem innocuous. When Google announced that it was building a server farm in Lenoir, North Carolina in March 2007, it had all the appearance of a feel-good story for a town whose traditional wooden furniture manufacturing industry had largely decamped to China. Aside from the impending strain on the electrical grid though (for which the North Carolina state government waived sales tax at Google's request) the state subsidies attracting Google broke down to an estimated $1.24 million per promised job, with very limited guarantees on sustained presence within the region other than that temporary opportunity to exploit underused power capacity.

for those with too much time on their hands and a sense of humour that tends towards the diabolical, the temptation to turn the tables on the scammers is too strong to resist. Often they will log the ensuing comic results on scambaiting websites such as 419 Eater or Artists against 419 — sites whose prevailing tone oscillates between a kind of disingenuously puritanical self-righteousness and a gleefully wicked encouragement of their members' exploits.

The organisers of these sites will claim a kind of vigilante public service in tying up the gangs with increasingly absurd replies and requests that mirror the delaying tactics the gangs employ to fleece their victims. So where the gangs will ask for an advance fee for administrative purposes, bribes or electronic banking details to get the promised millions out of the country (offering ever more elaborate and tortured excuses as they fleece their victim), the scambaiters will feign interest, as our American has done, then FedEx the gang a brick in lieu of bank documents at the gang's expense, ask them to photograph themselves holding up a paper sign (usually spelling out a very unflattering verdict on the bearer) or even, in an echo of the origin of the term 'spam' in a Monty Python sketch, have them make YouTube videos of themselves complaining about dead parrots.[12]

Whatever the methods, it's a peculiar pathology that seems to drive this activity and one that speaks to a definite lag and certain tensions in the globalising world. The access to communication technology that shrinks the world enough to make these appeals possible also reveals the ugly vigour of their

12 In the late 1980s, users of bulletin boards would routinely abuse newcomers unfamiliar with the etiquette and in-jokes of a forum by repeating the phrase 'Spam' onscreen until the newcomers comments were scrolled off the bottom of the screen — an homage to the Monty Python sketch in which a waitress in a British café offers various 'options' dominated by repeated instances of tinned Spam ('Spam, Spam, Spam, Spam, chips and Spam', etc). This is commonly believed to be the origin of the term 'spam' (and the Monty Python link gives it good geek pedigree), though various other largely discredited claims persist — from the presumption that, like so many other Internet phenomena, it must be an acronym ('shit posing as mail') to the belief that it stems from the Esperanto term 'spamo', derived from 'senpete alsendita mesâgo', 'a message sent without request'. The Hormel company, which has manufactured Spam (a contraction of 'spiced ham') since 1937, have intermittently attempted to enforce their trademark with limited success — they have thus far only been able to make cases against companies using the upper-case spelling of the word.

rebuttals — perhaps issued in fear that the movement of data precedes a movement of people.[13]

Whatever the reasons behind the sheer number and intensity of the responses,
it's clear from looking through the archives (or 'trophy room', as one site has it) of
these websites that the counter-pranks they record throw up as many unimagina-
tive redundancies as there are in the original con letters, as well as creating a cumu-
lative effect of boorishness and casual racism through the underlying assumption
and expression of 'natural' superiority (fuelled by nothing more than the economic
and technological access privileges of geographical birthright). The exchange
between the American and the Nigerian that forms the basis of this text is only one
of countless exchanges whose very public recording just shows a different side of
the coin of the same victim's vanity that drives a successful con.

I singled out this exchange for the ironic aptness of the American image (a post-
card from the saccharine heart of the dreamworld) and the way that its coupling
with the Nigerian responses to it perhaps serves as metaphor for other relation-
ships — the fair uses that give the title to this book project. *Legal Action* is one of several images of the same celebrities painted by Consani under license from the dead
stars' estates — legal agreements duly noted in the small print at the bottom of the
reproductions of these paintings. Like the popular search terms that algorithms
harvest and deploy in certain tropes of spam e-mails to get past the mail program's
filters, these groupings of Dean, Presley, Monroe, et al. provide some inadvertent
gauge of the culture that spawned them — inspired as they are by a machine-like,
if/then, aggregate assessment of what people want ('If people love Elvis and people love Marilyn, then people will really love Elvis and Marilyn. And if people
really love Elvis and Marilyn and people love James Dean . . .') This synthetic,

---

13 In their own way, the scambaiters have much in common with groups such as the TechnoPatriots
— an online equivalent of the civilian militia the Minutemen, who patrol the border between
Mexico and the U.S. to prevent illegal immigrants from crossing. The TechnoPatriots, who claim
to have members as far flung as New York, carry out the same task by monitoring online web-
cams mounted on mobile homes and and telegraph poles on private land in Arizona — calling in
suspicious movement as it stop-frames across their windows.

undiluted flavour of mid-twentieth-century American cultural hegemony might be kitsch, but it also speaks to the power of that moment and its persistent aura(s). It's a power that's much altered if not entirely diminished at the moment in which a dial-up connection is made in Lagos, a message routed through Reston, Virginia and a silent broadband download is delivered to a man living in the heart of the spectacular economy.

It seems only fair to ask similar questions of that man and his choice of image as we posed about the intentions of the Nigerian and his degrees of mask play as his photo was taken.[14] It's an image that implicates the sender as much as his target. Whatever his degree of ironic detachment, whatever distance he feels he has travelled from the moment when the images of Elvis Presley, Humphrey Bogart, Marilyn Monroe and James Dean might have been celebrated as uncomplicated ciphers of glamour in his own milieu (presumably, part of the condescending humour of the prank depends on a belief that those ciphers still hold their 'worth' in Nigeria), the man still settled on this image to send as a legitimised representation of his culture.

Perhaps it's stoner humour. The ad he placed for a roommate specified 'occasional 420' — 420 being a vernacular code of indeterminate origin signifying marijuana use. The adjacency of this numerical code for opting out, downtime, dulling the senses, to the persistent scattershot scam appeals marked by the number 419 has always struck me as poetically apt.[15] Since 2005, I have been logging Google alerts for '419 scam' and 'occasional 420' — each online use of either phrase triggering an e-mail to my inbox. With few exceptions I've long since stopped reading the contents of the alerts themselves, but they mark a repetitive tempo within the rhythms of my inbox that I've become attached to. The 419 alerts are a fairly constant tattoo and, should I so wish, I could follow the links back,

14 With due deference to the Turing test, I'm calling the American a man, less in acknowledgement that any linguistic clues confirm gender than the fact that his activities suggest a kind of absurd territorial pissing.

15 A nod here to Golan Levin's electronic artwork on this theme, *Secret Life of Numbers* from 2002, http://www.turbulence.org/Works/nums/prepare.html.

mostly to existing blog entries written by American commentators, local news journalists or tech advisers, speaking to a steady stream of scam attempts flowing into the country. The 420 alerts come through at a slower pace but are regular nonetheless — though most disappear (in smoke?) within a few days of appearing, as rooms are taken and online ads removed. Ads that speak of no drama, central locations and free WiFi. Lifestyles to be aspired to and, it seems, protected.

The American may try to persist with the prank — see how far he can push an absurd premise in the name of humour. Should he choose to prolong the circuit of deceit and send a return e-mail, it will find itself routed not through a countryside server farm but through an urban area such as Lagos or Port Harcourt. The electricity grid in Nigeria, let alone the communications network, is largely concentrated in these large urban centres and those pockets of land which are currently being actively exploited by oil companies.[16]

16 To talk about Nigeria's relationship to computer technology without talking about oil is impossible. The first wildcat drillers appeared in the Niger delta area in 1951 — the year after Turing published *Computing Machinery and Intelligence* (which included his description of the 'Imitation Game'). By the time the first crude oil exports left Port Harcourt in 1958, one of the more egregious examples of corporate rapaciousness via technology was well under way. In the now-familiar pattern that marks neoliberal investment logic, companies such as Shell and Chevron installed pipelines and infrastructure (including communication technology and the exponential growth of English as the language of business) for as long as it took to extract worth from the land and no more. They would then withdraw to the next field — leaving a trail of badly capped wells, pollution, disease and poverty in their wake. The desire within capitalism for frictionless, 'well-oiled' accumulation of capital, an imperative urge that must move where it wishes whatever the human cost, is well documented elsewhere, but the Nigerian experience is a particularly ugly and salutary one — according to Berkeley scholar and oil-industry specialist Michael Watts, when oil was discovered in Mongolia, a local leader cautioned that they did not want to become another Nigeria. Shell's violent protection of its interest also has sparked armed resistance from a group calling itself MEND (featuring a charismatic spokesman — most likely several people — called Jomo Gbomo, whose numerous electronic communications have been compared to those of Subcomandante Marcos of the Zapatistas) who claim to have shut in around 900,000 barrels a day of Nigeria's oil production — around 40% of the country's total output. For a more thorough overview on the Nigerian delta experience and MEND, I recommend Watts' and photojournalist Ed Kashi's book *Curse of the Black Gold* (2008). It's worth noting, though, that just as the injustices, graft culture and highly visible inequalities driven by Nigerian industry and government give rise to the potential for such resistance, they also arguably give rise to the culture that allows the 419 con to breed and thrive.

Whilst it may not have the network of server farms that mark the U.S. seaboard, Nigeria does possess equivalent 'foundations' – a large, and indeed largely unregulated, collection of landfill sites filled with discarded U.S. technology. The technology is sent to Nigeria in deals negotiated with notoriously corrupt government officials, nominally to provide computers to schools and hospitals that may be obsolete under the Moore's law logic of U.S. standards, but that should be perfectly serviceable for the tasks they are sent for.[17] Unfortunately, the machines routinely arrive with hard drives missing or broken beyond repair – rendering them unusable and fit only for landfill (a condition tacitly understood by all parties in the transaction). Photos taken by the activist group the Basel Action Network show piles of defunct machines in shipping crates that end up obscenely pockmarking swampland and residential areas alike.[18] In confirmation of the technologies' origins, activists have occasionally found working, undeleted hard drives on these discarded machines containing outgoing e-mail records from, say, World Bank officials.

This continuous flow of and selective disregard for 'trash' demonstrates yet one more ironic mirroring within a perverse 'ecosystem' of masked physical and virtual exchanges between Nigeria and America – in the spectral spirit of capitalism's tendency to conceal one set of operations within the appearance of another. It's a mirroring to match that of the symbolic desires, values and projections upon the other that mark the scammers on both sides, in which spam e-mails might be seen as a kind of trace element of the myriad transactions, frauds and inequalities that mark globalisation.

Perhaps the American does send another message, conceived behind a smirk in a private room lit by an LCD glow and dispatched with silent broadband

---

17 An assertion originally made by Intel co-founder Gordon E. Moore in 1965 (revised in 1975) that the number of transistors that could be inexpensively placed on a single microchip would effectively double every two years. The rule has held till the present day and is expected to remain true for the next decade. The consistency of the rule and the regular doubling of processing power it describes has effectively set the tempo for everything from computer industry financial forecasts to the corollary cycles of built-in obsolescence (and thus disposal strategies).

18 See www.ban.org. Named for the 1994 Basel Convention on the disposal of toxic waste.

speed and efficiency (the rotating clock icon onscreen reverting to a regular cursor in a barely discernible second). Perhaps it reaches the young man in Nigeria, with the text downloading in a noticeable dial-up stagger to the chaotic agora of a Lagos call shop. Perhaps the masquerade exchange will continue indefinitely at the same lopsided tempo, with the same lopsided routing and diversions of power, whilst the respective landfills swell and Moore's law holds good . . .

if/then . . .

I don suffer no be small
Upon say I get sense
Poverty no good at all, no
Na im make I join this business
419 no be thief, its just a game
Everybody dey play am

ILLUSTRATIONS

PETROL LIAR

NARROW GAUGE

419 (*occasional* 420)

THE WIRE

SPECTRES OF MARKS

PETROL LIAR

MANCHESTER

2001

vent: an apple with two bites (or possibly bytes) out of it and rainbow colors that code for homosext

, and in a fit of depression, Turing committed suicide in June of 1954 by eating a cyanide-poisoned a

e 7, 1954, despondent over his situation, Turing committed suicide by eating an apple laced with cya

There is also Alan Turing's poisoned a

Finally, in June of 1954, Turing ate an apple poisoned by cyanide and ended his ow

On June 7, 1954, he committed suicide by eating an apple laced with cya

lan Turing took a bite of a poison apple when commiting suicide, and the name was picked as an ho

alike, British mathematician Alan Turing committed suicide in 1954 by biting into a cyanide-laced a

n: He instead ate a cyanide-laced apple in homage to a favorite movie, Snow White and the Seven D

nes of knowledge plus recalling Turing's last supper and evoking Newton, founder of science-as-num

atment that made him impotent and obese, Alan Turing eats an apple dipped in cyanide and dies, age

He died on 7 June 1954, presumably a suicide by eating an apple laced with potassium cya

nized mathematics, helped the British crack secret Nazi codes and died after biting into a poisoned a

ound dead with that apple, an apparent suicide committed by a man who had had a thing for Snow W

And, in a curious echo of this film, Turing killed himself by eating a poisoned a

He dipped an apple in cyanide and

- intend to take his life when, to dramatize a point for his class, he dipped an apple in potassium cya

w where I read it) is that he chose a poisoned apple because Snow White had been his favourite fairy

me in on 8 June 1954. He had died the day before of cyanide poisoning, a half-eaten apple beside his

gen had terrible side effects, and fifty years ago this month, Alan Turing poisoned an apple and bit d

ain that Turing had committed suicide at the age of 42 by taking a bite from an apple laced with cya

e. One night, prior to eating his apple he decided to inject it with cyanide. Alan Turing committed sui

s of public exposure which led him to take his own life – by eating an apple laced with cyanide – in

soned apple, the meaning of the Apple Computer logo, Adam and Eve as forbidden fruit, and much n

g medical treatment that he had been forced to undergo (in lieu of prison) to 'cure' him of homosexua

o suicide, the rainbow apple with bytes missing for the Apple Mac symbol is actually a homage to Tu

dipped into cyanide (not found in his house) and Alan Turing's mouth dipped into the apple several ti

s perhaps more than the hormone treatment was the background to his suicide by eating a poisoned a

Turing died by his own hand in 1954 by eating an apple dipped in strych

with cyanide. It has been suggested that Apple Macintosh computers were so named in tribute to Tu

partly eaten apple — has continued to haunt the intellectual Eden from which Alan Turing was expe

ring was found dead on 7 June 1954 during a period in which he was conducting electrolysis experim

e. Anyways he was killed by a poisoned apple. He was found dead in his room with a bite taken out

Turing died in 1954 by biting into an apple he had previously poiso

ne, 1954, Alan Turing lay down on his bed, took a bite from an apple, dipped it in cyanide, and bit a

a reference to Alan Turing, as one of the fathers of modern computing, who died eating a poisoned a

symbolism) and how she is reminded of him every time she sees the rainbow apple of apple compute

ium cyanide poisoning on June 7, 1954. The cyanide was found on a partially eaten apple next to his

which lead to Turing killing himself with a cyanide laden a

a. Died of cyanide poisoning; half-eaten apple by him b. Coroner concluded was suicide (mom disag

alently, his loss of confidence in them, might well have sufficed to induce him to choose the nearest

eath and destiny of the man who did so much to decipher the Enigma code during the Second World

He killed himself by eating a apple soaked in potassium cyan

In 1954 he committed suicide by eating a poisonous apple laced with cya

Turing died in 1954 of eating an apple that had been poisoned with potassium cyan

tted suicide by eating a cyanide-laced apple, hoping that his mother would believe that it was an acci

The official theory is that he died by eating a cyanide-poisoned app

On 7 June 1954, in Wilslow, England, Turing commits suicide by eating a cyanide laced ap

th nor that he ate a deliberately-poisoned apple (potassium cyanide being the toxic agent) to do himse

venenamiento with cyanide, apparently after eating a poisoned apple that did not get to ingest comple

1954, Alan Turing was found dead by his cleaning lady, a half-eaten apple dipped in cyanide by his

in the role of the innocent girl: Dorothy, Alice, and ultimately Snow White biting on the poisoned ap

our age laid down in his Spartan bed, crunched down on an apple laced with potassium cyanide, and d

ly that Apple's logo was designed not to honor forbidden fruit but to commemorate Alan Turing's suic

a bite from an apple coated with cyanide (the rainbow also being a symbol of homosexuality at the ti

dead by his cleaner on June 8, 1954. He had died of cyanide poisoning, a half-eaten apple beside his

holding an apple was finally winched down to a waiting plinth in Sackville Park in the city centre to

ity, he next mimicked Snow White: "Turing ended his life in 1954 by eating an apple dipped in cyani

ter being harassed for his homosexuality. He did this by taking a 'byte' from an apple laced with cyan

entators believe, however, that he committed suicide by eating an apple smeared with cyanide-laced

uite possible that there was some cyanide on his hands as he ate, so his death may have been an accid

Cook several apple rings at a time in butter, turing once, until golden bro

soned apple, the meaning of the Apple Computer logo